Table of Contents

Executive Summary

This report analyzes the most recent, reliable data about rape and sexual assault in our country. It identifies those most at risk of being victims of these crimes, examines the cost of this violence (both to survivors and our communities), and describes the response, too often inadequate, of the criminal justice system. The report catalogues steps this Administration has taken to combat rape and sexual assault, and identifies areas for further action.

An overview of the problem:

- **Women and girls are the vast majority of victims**: nearly 1 in 5 women – or nearly 22 million – have been raped in their lifetimes.[1]
- **Men and boys, however, are also at risk**: 1 in 71 men – or almost 1.6 million – have been raped during their lives.
- **Women of all races are targeted, but some are more vulnerable than others:** 33.5% of multiracial women have been raped, as have 27% of American Indian and Alaska Native women, compared to 15% of Hispanic, 22% of Black, and 19% of White women.
- **Most victims know their assailants.**
- **The vast majority (nearly 98%) of perpetrators are male.**
- **Young people are especially at risk:** nearly half of female survivors were raped before they were 18, and over one-quarter of male survivors were raped before they were 10. College students are particularly vulnerable: 1 in 5 women has been sexually assaulted while in college.
- **Repeat victimization is common:** over a third of women who were raped as minors were also raped as adults.

Other populations are also at higher risk of being raped or sexually assaulted, including people with disabilities, the LGBT community, prison inmates (of both genders), and the homeless. Undocumented immigrants face unique challenges, because their abusers often threaten to have them deported if they try to get help.

---

[1] Black, M.C., Basile, K.C., Breiding, M.J., Smith, S.G., Walters, M.L., Merrick, M.T., Chen, J., & Stevens, M.R. (2011). *The National Intimate Partner and Sexual Violence Survey (NISVS): 2010 Summary Report.* Atlanta, GA: National Center for Injury Prevention and Control, Centers for Disease Control and Prevention.

In calculating the prevalence of rape, The Centers for Disease Control and Prevention (CDC) counts completed forced penetration, attempted forced penetration, or alcohol/drug facilitated completed penetration. Like other researchers, the CDC considers attempted forced penetration to fall within the definition of "rape" because that crime can be just as traumatizing for victims. As the CDC further explains, the most common form of rape victimization experienced by women was completed forced penetration: 12.3% of women in the United States were victims of completed forced penetration; 8% were victims of alcohol/drug-facilitated completed penetration, and 5.2% were victims of attempted forced penetration. These are lifetime estimates and a victim might have experienced multiple forms of these subtypes of rape in her lifetime.

The Impacts of Rape and Sexual Assault. Rape and sexual assault survivors often suffer from a wide range of physical and mental health problems that can follow them for life – including depression, chronic pain, diabetes, anxiety, eating disorders, and post-traumatic stress disorder. They are also more likely than non-victims to attempt or consider suicide.

The Economic Costs. Although hard to quantify, several studies have calculated the economic costs of a rape, accounting for medical and victim services, loss of productivity, decreased quality of life, and law enforcement resources. Each used a slightly different methodology, but all found the costs to be significant: ranging from $87,000 to $240,776 per rape.

Campus Sexual Assault: A Particular Problem. As noted, 1 in 5 women has been sexually assaulted while she's in college. The dynamics of college life appear to fuel the problem, as many victims are abused while they're drunk, under the influence of drugs, passed out, or otherwise incapacitated. Most college victims are assaulted by someone they know – and parties are often the site of these crimes. Notably, campus assailants are often serial offenders: one study found that of the men who admitted to committing rape or attempted rape, some 63% said they committed an average of six rapes each. College sexual assault survivors suffer from high levels of mental health problems (like depression and PTSD) and drug and alcohol abuse. Reporting rates are also particularly low.

The Criminal Justice Response. Despite the prevalence of rape and sexual assault, many offenders are neither arrested nor prosecuted. A number of factors may contribute to low arrest rates – but police biases (e.g., believing that many victims falsely claim rape to get attention, or that only those who've been physically injured are telling the truth) persist, and may account for some officers' unwillingness to make an arrest. Also, the trauma that often accompanies a sexual assault can leave a victim's memory and verbal skills impaired – and without trauma-sensitive interviewing techniques, a women's initial account can sometimes seem fragmented.

Even when arrests are made, prosecutors are often reluctant to take on rape and sexual assault cases – and, in some jurisdictions, the backlog of untested rape kits can also be a factor in low prosecution rates. Rape kits – which collect forensic evidence of a rape or sexual assault, including the perpetrator's DNA – can be vital to successful prosecutions. Once tested, an offender's DNA can be matched with other offender samples in the FBI's national database, thus identifying assailants and linking crimes together. Unfortunately, however, many rape kits are still sitting on the shelves, either ignored or waiting to be tested.

Responding to the President's 2010 call to action, the Administration is aggressively working to combat rape and sexual assault on many fronts. For example:

- Last year, the President signed the third reauthorization of the Violence Against Women Act – the backbone of our nation's response to violence against women, authored and pioneered by then-Senator Joe Biden – which commits unprecedented resources to breaking the cycle of sexual violence. Among other measures, VAWA 2013:

  - o Includes set-aside funding for multidisciplinary sexual assault teams; these are specially trained units of detectives, prosecutors, healthcare providers and victim advocates, all working together to support sexual assault survivors and increase the odds of successful prosecutions. These teams have a proven track record of winning convictions and helping survivors get back on their feet.

  - o Provides new funding for sexual assault nurse examiners (SANEs), who are specially trained to provide respectful and supportive care while collecting forensic evidence after a rape or sexual assault. Here, too, research shows that the work of these nurses both improves victim care and increases rates of successful prosecutions.

  - o Funds specialized training for law enforcement officers and prosecutors – so they can learn how to conduct trauma-informed interviews and investigations, and more effectively bring offenders to justice.

  - o Includes new protections for LGBT, immigrant, and Native American victims, as well as for those who live in low-income or subsidized housing.

The Administration has also:

- Undertaken a major effort to make our colleges and universities safer – by issuing guidance to help schools understand their obligations to prevent and respond to campus sexual assault, and by stepping up federal compliance and enforcement actions.

- Adopted a series of Executive Actions to address sexual assault in the military – including measures to improve command accountability, expand victims' rights within the military justice system, increase training across the ranks, and provide new support for victims. Notably, Secretary Hagel directed each service to provide all victims of sexual assault with legal counsel, who will be at a victim's side at every step of the process.

- Successfully called on Congress to double funding for VAWA's Sexual Assault Services Program (SASP), the first funding stream to focus specifically on rape and sexual assault. SASP provides for a wide array of services, such as crisis intervention, counseling, rape crisis centers, medical and social services, 24-hour sexual assault hotlines, and medical and legal advocacy.

- Launched the **1 is 2 Many** Campaign to focus on teen and young-adult sexual violence. Among a number of other initiatives, the Campaign inspired creation of the "Circle of 6" app – which puts a group of friends instantly in touch with each other, so someone in trouble can send a "come and get me" message, complete with a GPS location map. The Campaign also developed best-practices resources on teen dating violence for schools, and convened a series of forums to enlist men in the effort to end violence against women.

- Secured funding for the National Dating Abuse Helpline to expand to digital services, which lets teens and young adults reach out for help in a way that they are most comfortable – via text messaging and online "chats."

- Modernized the definition of "rape" for nationwide data collection, ensuring a more accurate account of the crime.

- Developed a national, best-practices protocol for conducting sexual assault forensic examinations.

- Developed a five-year strategic plan to address the tragedy of human trafficking, especially as it impacts runaway, homeless and LGBT youth.

- Funded projects to reduce the rape kit backlog, with some impressive results.

- Directed all federal agencies to develop polices to address domestic violence, sexual assault and stalking in the federal workforce.

- Implemented a series of major initiatives to protect American Indian and Alaska Native Women, including more resources for tribal law enforcement, court systems, and victim services; new penalties for spouse and intimate-partner violence; and expanded jurisdiction to allow both federal and tribal authorities to hold domestic abusers, whether Indian or non-Indian, accountable.

- Developed a 56-point action agenda for federal agencies to address the link between violence against women and HIV/AIDS.

- Promulgated new guidelines requiring prisons and other detention facilities to prevent, detect, and respond to sexual assault.

The Administration is committed to redoubling the work it is already doing. At the same time, it is also exploring new frontiers.

Continuing to Focus on Campus Sexual Assault. To make our campuses safer, change still needs to come from many quarters: schools must adopt better policies and practices to prevent these crimes and to more effectively respond when they happen. And federal agencies must ensure that schools are living up to their obligations. To accomplish these and other goals, the President today is establishing a White House Task Force to Protect Students from Sexual Assault. The Task Force will:

- Provide educational institutions with best practices for preventing and responding to rape and sexual assault.
- Build on the federal government's enforcement efforts to ensure that educational institutions comply fully with their legal obligations.
- Improve transparency of the government's enforcement activities.
- Increase the public's awareness of an institution's track record in addressing rape and sexual assault.
- Enhance coordination among federal agencies to hold schools accountable if they do not confront sexual violence on their campuses.

Increasing Arrest, Prosecution and Conviction Rates. Across all demographics, rapists and sex offenders are too often not made to pay for their crimes, and remain free to assault again. Arrest rates are low and meritorious cases are still being dropped – many times because law enforcement officers and prosecutors are not fully trained on the nature of these crimes or how best to investigate and prosecute them. Many new and promising interviewing, investigative and prosecution protocols are being developed, with cutting-edge science about victim trauma informing the enterprise. We need to further develop these best practices and help get them out to the field.

We can also help local jurisdictions move rape kits off the shelves and into crime labs for testing – so more rapists can be identified through DNA and brought to justice.

Committing Vital Resources. This Administration has made an unparalleled commitment to getting victims and survivors the many services they need – from crisis intervention, counseling, legal advocacy, medical help, social services, and job and housing assistance – and with a special eye on particularly vulnerable populations. We cannot retreat, but must recommit to getting these vital resources to those who need them.

Changing the Culture. Sexual assault is pervasive because our culture still allows it to persist. According to the experts, violence prevention can't just focus on the perpetrators and the survivors. It has to involve everyone. And in order to put an end to this violence, we as a nation must see it for what it is: a crime. Not a misunderstanding, not a private matter, not anyone's right or any woman's fault. And bystanders must be taught and emboldened to step in to stop it. We can only stem the tide of violence if we all do our part.

Introduction

The numbers alone are stunning: nearly 1 in 5 women – or almost 22 million – have been raped in their lifetimes.

And the numbers don't begin to tell the whole story. They don't tell of the physical, emotional and psychological scars that a victim can carry for life. They don't speak to the betrayal and broken trust when the attacker is a friend, a trusted colleague, or a family member. And they don't give voice to the courage of survivors who work every day to put their lives back together.

Twenty years ago, then-Senator Joe Biden authored the Violence Against Women Act (VAWA) to bring the problem of domestic violence and sexual assault out from the shadows and into the national spotlight. In the intervening decades, help has come: rape crisis centers have been built; hotlines are up and running; dedicated activists, advocates and service providers have more resources; states have passed tough new laws; and more abusers and sex offenders have been put behind bars.

In 2010, President Obama called upon all federal agencies to make domestic and sexual violence a priority. And in March 7, 2013, he signed the third reauthorization of VAWA, which provides states, tribes, and local communities with unprecedented resources to combat sexual assault. This and other federal programs put federal dollars where they are most needed and effective: for crisis intervention, counseling, criminal justice advocacy, forensic evidence-gathering, medical and social services, law enforcement training and prosecutorial resources. In 2012, President Obama directed federal agencies to develop policies to address domestic violence, sexual assault, and stalking in the federal workplace.

Federal agencies have heeded the President's call to action in many innovative and wide-ranging ways. Among other initiatives, the Administration has issued new guidance to help schools, colleges and universities better understand their obligations to prevent and respond to sexual assault on their campuses; promulgated a series of executive actions to better protect our service members from military sexual assault; developed a national, best-practices protocol for conducting sexual assault forensic examinations; modernized the definition of "rape" for nationwide data collection, ensuring a more accurate accounting of the crime; launched new technologically-advanced ways for young women to get help; and enlisted men and boys to take an active stand against sexual violence. And today, the President is establishing a White House Task Force to Protect Students from Sexual Assault – which will go even further to make our schools safer for all students.

More of the Administration's efforts are catalogued in this report – and they are making a real difference.

But despite all the progress, too many of our friends, wives, sisters, daughters and sons are still raped or sexually assaulted every day.

A new generation of anti-rape activists, both women and men, are having a national conversation about rape and sexual assault – and about attitudes toward victims and the role of the criminal justice system in holding offenders accountable.

This report aims to be part of that conversation. It provides an overview of the scope of the problem, identifies those most at risk, describes the costs of this violence (both to survivors and society as a whole), and takes a look at the response of the criminal justice system. The report discusses steps this Administration has taken to address rape and sexual assault, and identifies challenging new fronts on which we should set our sights.[2]

---

[2] The terms "survivor" and "victim" are both used to describe individuals who have been raped or sexually assaulted. Many of these individuals and the advocates who work with them have come to prefer "survivor," as they regard the term as more empowering. The term "victim," however, is still in widespread use in research studies and in the criminal justice context. In this report, the terms are used interchangeably and always with respect for those who have suffered from these crimes.

An Overview of the Problem

Anyone can be a victim of rape or sexual assault. But some are more at risk than others:

- **Women and girls are the vast majority of victims**: as noted, nearly 1 in 5 women has been raped in her lifetime.[3]

- **Men and boys, however, are also at risk**: 1 in 71 men – or almost 1.6 million – have been raped during their lives.[4]

- **Women of all races are targeted, but some are more vulnerable than others:** 33.5% of multiracial women have been raped, as have 27% of American Indian and Alaska Native women, compared to 15% of Hispanic, 22% of Black, and 19% of White women.[5]

- **Most victims know their perpetrators:** 51% of female victims were raped by a current or former intimate partner, and 41% were raped by an acquaintance. Stranger rape, in contrast, accounts for 14% of the total.[6] Of men and boys, 52% report being raped by an acquaintance and 15% by a stranger.[7]

- **Repeat victimization is common:** over a third of women who were raped as minors were also raped as adults.[8]

- **The majority of perpetrators are male:** 98% of female and 93% of male rape survivors report that their assailants were male.[9]

- **Young people are especially at risk:** nearly half of female survivors were raped before they were 18, and over one-quarter of male survivors were raped before they were 10.[10]

---

[3] Black, M.C., Basile, K.C., Breiding, M.J., Smith, S.G., Walters, M.L., Merrick, M.T., Chen, J., & Stevens, M.R. (2011). *The National Intimate Partner and Sexual Violence Survey (NISVS): 2010 Summary Report.* Atlanta, GA: National Center for Injury Prevention and Control, Centers for Disease Control and Prevention. [Hereafter cited as NISVS (2010)] In calculating the prevalence of rape, The Centers for Disease Control and Prevention (CDC) counts completed forced penetration, attempted forced penetration, or alcohol/drug facilitated completed penetration. Like other researchers, the CDC considers attempted forced penetration to fall within the definition of "rape" because that crime can be just as traumatizing for victims. As the CDC further explains, the most common form of rape victimization experienced by women was completed forced penetration: 12.3% of women in the United States were victims of completed forced penetration; 8% were victims of alcohol/drug-facilitated completed penetration, and 5.2% were victims of attempted forced penetration.   These are lifetime estimates and a victim might have experienced multiple forms of these subtypes of rape in her lifetime.

[4] NISVS (2010)

[5] NISVS (2010); Asian or Pacific Islander (API) women are also assaulted. However, the NISVS does not report the prevalence of sexual violence for API women due to a high standard error or low number of responses.

[6] Some women are raped by multiple perpetrators in different relationships. Because a woman may be raped both by an intimate partner and a stranger, the overall percentages do not sum to 100.

[7] NISVS (2010)

[8] NISVS (2010)

[9] NISVS (2010)

[10] NISVS (2010)

A Closer Look at the Demographics

Teens and young adults. The majority of rape and sexual assault victims are young – between the ages of 16 and 24. The Centers for Disease Control and Prevention (CDC) reports that 80% of female victims were raped before they turned 25, and almost half were raped before they were 18.[11] Among men, 28% were raped before they were 10.[12]

Some 12% of high school girls report having been forced to have sexual intercourse.[13] And up to 38% of runaway teens say that sexual abuse is one of the reasons they left home.[14]

College students are especially at risk: 1 in 5 women has been sexually assaulted while in college.[15]

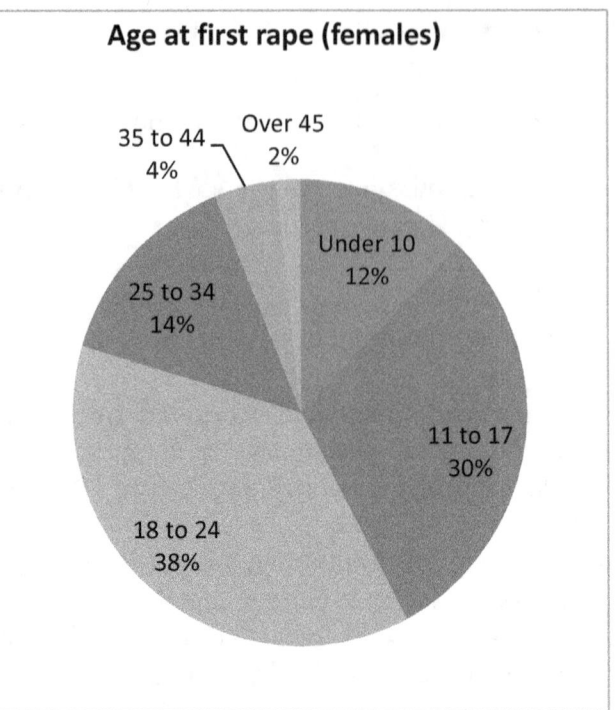

Age at first rape (females)

- 35 to 44 — 4%
- Over 45 — 2%
- Under 10 — 12%
- 25 to 34 — 14%
- 11 to 17 — 30%
- 18 to 24 — 38%

People with disabilities. People with physical or mental disabilities may also be at increased risk. A study found that in the mid-1990s, women with severe disabilities were four times more likely to be sexually assaulted than women with no disability.[16] A more recent study made similar findings, reporting that individuals with a disability were three times more likely to be raped or sexually assaulted than individuals without a disability.[17]

LGBT community. People who identify as lesbian, gay, bisexual, or transgender (LGBT) are also uniquely vulnerable. One study found that 13.2% of bisexual men and 11.6% of gay men were raped in adulthood, compared to 1.6% of heterosexual men.[18] According to the CDC, 46% of bisexual women have been raped, compared to 13% of lesbians and

---

[11] NISVS (2010)

[12] NISVS (2010); "Age at first rape (females)" chart is derived from NISVS (2010). A comparable breakdown for males is not available because NIVIS (2010) does not report any age categories for males, other than "under 10."

[13] *Youth Risk Behavior Surveillance*. (2011). Centers for Disease Control and Prevention. U.S. Department of Health and Human Services.

[14] Greene, J., & Sanchez, R. (2002). *Sexual Abuse Among Homeless Adolescents: Prevalence, Correlates and Sequelea*. The Administration on Children, Youth and Families.

[15] Krebs, C. P., Lindquist, C. H., Warner, T. D., Fisher, B. S., & Martin, S. L. (2007). *The Campus Sexual Assault (CSA) Study* (221153). Washington, DC: National Institute of Justice, U.S. Department of Justice. [Hereafter cited as CSA (2007)].; Krebs, C. P., Lindquist, C. H., Warner, T. D., Fisher, B. S., & Martin, S. L (2009) College Women's Experiences with Physically Forced, Alcohol- or Other Drug-Enabled, and Drug-Facilitated Sexual Assault Before and Since Entering College. *Journal of American College Health, 57*(6), 639-647.

[16] Casteel, C., Martin, S. L., Smith, J. B., Gurka, K. K., & Kupper, L. L. (2008). National study of physical and sexual assault among women with disabilities. *Injury Prevention, 14*(2), 87-90.

[17] Harrell, E. (2012). *Crime Against Persons with Disabilities, 2009-2011 – Statistical Tables*. Bureau of Justice Statistics, U.S. Department of Justice.

[18] Balsam, K. F., Beauchaine, T. P., & Rothblum, E. D. (2005). Victimization over the life span: A comparison of lesbian, gay, bisexual, and heterosexual siblings. *Journal of Consulting and Clinical Psychology, 73*(3), 477-487. [Hereafter cited as Balsam (2005)]

17% of heterosexual women.[19] Another study found that more than 25% of transgender individuals had been sexually assaulted after the age of 13.[20]

Incarcerated individuals. Sexual assault is a problem in our nation's prisons. Among former state prisoners, 14% of females and 4% of males were sexually assaulted by another prisoner. Incarcerated gay and bisexual men are at particular risk: 34% of bisexual males and 39% of gay males report being sexually assaulted by another prisoner, compared to 3.5% of heterosexual males.[21]

Undocumented immigrants. While numbers are difficult to estimate, undocumented immigrants face unique difficulties. Abusers often threaten to have their victims deported if they try to seek help, making immigrant survivors less likely to report these crimes.[22] Immigrant survivors may also be unaware or confused by the services that are available, particularly if service providers lack linguistically or culturally appropriate resources.[23]

People who are homeless. There's a correlation between homelessness and sexual violence. One study found that 13% of homeless women had been raped in the previous year, and half of these women were raped at least twice.[24] This compares to 1% of women nationally who reported being raped in the previous year.[25] Additionally, up to 43% of homeless women were abused as children.[26]

[19] Walters, M.L., Chen, J., & Breiding, M.J. (2013). The National Intimate Partner and Sexual Violence Survey (NISVS): 2010 Findings on Victimization by Sexual Orientation. National Center for Injury Prevention and Control, Centers for Disease Control and Prevention.

[20] Testa, R. J., Sciacca, L. M., Wang, F., Hendricks, M. L., Goldblum, P., Bradford, J., & Bongar, B. (2012). Effects of Violence on Transgender People. *Professional Psychology: Research and Practice, 43*(5), 452-459.

[21] Beck, A.J. & Johnson, C. (2012). *Sexual Victimization Reported by Former State Prisoners, 2008.* Bureau of Justice Statistics, U.S. Department of Justice. Retrieved from http://www.prearesourcecenter.org/sites/default/files/library/sexualvictimizationreportedbyformerstateprisoners2008.pdf.

[22] Orloff, L.E. & Dave, N. (1997) Identifying Barriers: Survey of Immigrant Women and Domestic Violence in the D.C. Metropolitan Area. *Poverty and Race. 6*(4) 9-10

[23] Mindlin, J., Orloff, J.E., Pochiraju, S., Baran, A., & Echavarria, E. (2013).*Dynamics of sexual assault and the implications for immigrant women.* National Immigrant Women's Advocacy Project. Retrieved from: http://niwaplibrary.wcl.american.edu/cultural-competency/dynamics-of-violence-against-immigrant-women.

[24] Wenzel, S.L., Leake, B.D., Gelberg, L. (2000). Health of homeless women with recent experiences of rape. *Journal of General Internal Medicine, 15*(4).265-269.

[25] NISVS (2010)

[26] The National Center on Family Homelessness (2007). *Violence in the lives of homeless women.* Retrieved from: http://www.councilofcollaboratives.org/files/fact_violence.pdf.

The Impacts of Rape and Sexual Assault

Rape and sexual assault can take a profound toll on survivors, who often suffer from a wide range of physical and mental health problems that can be long-lasting.

Physical Health

According to the National Crime Victimization Survey, between 2005-2010, 58% of all female victims of sexual assault sustained an injury.[27] Women who are raped or stalked by any perpetrator or physically assaulted by an intimate partner are more likely to have asthma, irritable bowel syndrome, and diabetes, and are also more likely to suffer from chronic pain, frequent headaches, and difficulty sleeping than non-victims.[28] A study of women in North Carolina indicated that survivors of sexual assault were more likely to smoke, to have high cholesterol and hypertension, and to be obese.[29] African American women ages 18-24 who are sexually assaulted are nearly five times more likely to test positive for a high-risk HPV infection. Also, survivors of intimate partner rape or sexual assault are more likely than non-victims to contract sexually-transmitted infections, and are also more likely to report HIV risk factors, such as unprotected sex, injection drug use and alcohol abuse.[30]

Mental Health

Survivors also suffer from a wide range of mental health problems, including depression, anxiety, and post-traumatic stress disorder (PTSD).[31] One study found that over half of survivors who were forcibly raped while under the influence of alcohol or drugs developed lifetime PTSD. These victims were also almost five times more likely to have lifetime major depressive episodes than non-victims.[32]

---

[27] Planty, M., Berzofsky, M., Krebs, C., Langton, L., & Smiley-McDonald, H. (2013). *Female victims of sexual violence, 1994-2010*. Washington, DC: U.S. Dept. of Justice, Office of Justice Programs, Bureau of Justice Statistics. [Hereafter cited as Planty (2013)]

[28] NISVS (2010)

[29] Cloutier, S., Martin, S. L., & Poole, C. (2002). Sexual assault among North Carolina women: prevalence and health risk factors. *Journal of Epidemiology and Community Health, 56*(4), 265-271.

[30] Wingood, G. M., Seth, P., DiClemente, R. J., & Robinson, L. S. (2009). Association of sexual abuse with incident high-risk human papilloma- virus infection among young African-American women. *Sexually Transmitted Disease, 36*(12), 784-786.; Bauer, H. M., Gibson, P., Hernandez, M., Kent, C., Klausner, K., & Bolan, G. (2002). Intimate partner violence and high-risk sexual behaviors among female patients with sexually transmitted diseases. *Sexually Transmitted Diseases, 29*(7), 411-416.; Centers for Disease Control and Prevention. (2008) Adverse Health Conditions and Health Risk Behaviors Associated with Intimate Partner Violence --- United States, 2005. *MMWR. 57*(5): 113-7. Retrieved from: http://www.cdc.gov/mmwr/preview/mmwrhtml/mm5705a1.htm; Lang, D.L., et al. (2011) Rape victimization and high risk sexual behaviors: longitudinal study of African-American adolescent females. Western Journal of Emergency Medicine. *12*(3), 333-342.

[31] Many people with PTSD have flashbacks, repeatedly reliving the traumatic event in their thoughts or sleep. People with PTSD also may startle easily, lose interest in things they used to enjoy, or become more aggressive. National Council on Disability (n.d.). *Section 3: Post Traumatic Stress Disorder (PTSD) and Traumatic Brain Injury (TBI)*. Retrieved from http://www.ncd.gov/publications/2009/March042009/section3; National Institute of Mental Health (n.d.). *Anxiety Disorders*. Retrieved from http://http://www.nimh.nih.gov/health/publications/anxiety-disorders/index.shtml

[32] Zinzow, H., Resnick, H., Amstadter, A., McCauley, M., Ruggiero, K., & Kilpatrick, D. (2012). Prevalence and risk of psychiatric disorders as a function of variant rape histories: Results from a national survey of women. *Social Psychiatry and Psychiatric Epidemiology, 47*(6), 893-902. [Hereafter cited as Zinzow (2012)]

Survivors of sexual assault are also more likely than non-victims to engage in risky behavior – such as substance and alcohol abuse, smoking, and high-risk HIV behavior.[33] Experts believe these are a means of coping with the trauma, or that victims are otherwise self-medicating. One study found that when controlling for previous substance abuse history, sexual assault survivors were more likely to abuse alcohol than women who were not assaulted.[34] Another study found that female veterans who experienced sexual trauma in the military were twice as likely to report substance abuse, PTSD, and anxiety than female veterans who were not assaulted.[35]

Sexual assault survivors are also more prone to developing eating disorders: one survey of undergraduates found that victims were seven times more likely to vomit or use laxatives to lose weight than non-victims.[36]

Survivors of rape and sexual assault are also more likely to attempt or consider suicide. Research has found that men who were sexually abused in childhood are twice as likely as non-victims to attempt suicide.[37] One study found that high school students who were raped were more likely to report suicidal ideation in the past 12 months than their non-victimized counterparts.[38] Another study reported that almost half of female veterans who were sexually assaulted in the military report suicide ideation.[39]

Today, victims may be further traumatized by social media – through which the details of an assault can "go viral." While this is an unresearched issue, a number of high profile sexual assault cases have drawn attention to this relatively new and disturbing dynamic.

---

[33] Cloutier, S., Martin, S. L., & Poole, C. (2002). Sexual assault among North Carolina women: prevalence and health risk factors. *Journal of Epidemiology and Community Health, 56*(4), 265-271.; Centers for Disease Control and Prevention. Adverse Health Conditions and Health Risk Behaviors Associated with Intimate Partner Violence --- United States, 2005. MMWR. 2008; 57(5): 113-7. Available at http://www.cdc.gov/mmwr/preview/mmwrhtml/mm5705a1.htm; Lang, D.L., et al. Rape victimization and high risk sexual behaviors: longitudinal study of African-American adolescent females. Western Journal of Emergency Medicine. 2011; 12(3).; Kilpatrick, D.G., Acierno, R., Resnick, H., Sounders, B.E., Best, C.L. (1997). A 2-Year Longitudinal Analysis of the Relationships Between Violent Assault and Substance Use in Women. *Journal of Consulting and Clinical Psychology, 65*(5), 834-847.

[34] Kilpatrick, D.G., Acierno, R., Resnick, H., Sounders, B.E., Best, C.L. (1997). A 2-Year Longitudinal Analysis of the Relationships Between Violent Assault and Substance Use in Women. *Journal of Consulting and Clinical Psychology, 65*(5), 834-847.

[35] Kimerling, R., Street, A., Pavao, J., Smith, M., Cronkite, R. C., Holmes, T. H., & Frayne, S. (2010). Military-related sexual trauma among veterans health administration patients returning from Afghanistan and Iraq. *American Journal of Public Health, 100*(8), 1409–1412.

[36] Fischer, S., Stojek, M., & Hartzell, E. (2010). Effects of multiple forms of childhood abuse and adult sexual assault on current eating disorder symptoms. *Eating Behaviors, 11*(3), 190-192.; Gidycz, C. A., Orchowski, L. M., King, C. R., & Rich, C. L. (2008). Sexual Victimization and Health-Risk Behaviors. A Prospective Analysis of College Women. *Journal of Interpersonal Violence, 23*(6), 744-763.

[37] Dube, Shanta R. (2005). Long-Term Consequences of Childhood Sexual Abuse by Gender of Victim. *American Journal of Preventive Medicine, 28*(5), 430 - 438-438.

[38] Basile, Lynberg, Simon, Arias, Brener, & Saltzman (2006). The Association between self reported lifetime history of forced sexual intercourse and recent health risk behaviors: Findings from the 2003 National Youth Risk Behavior Survey. *Journal of Adolescent Health, 39*(5), 752.e1-752.e7 (available on-line only).

[39] Surís, A., Link-Malcolm, J., & North, C. S. (2011). Predictors of suicidal ideation in veterans with PTSD related to military sexual trauma. *Journal of Traumatic Stress, 24*(5), 605-608.

Campus Sexual Assault: A Particular Problem

Sexual assault is a particular problem on college campuses: 1 in 5 women has been sexually assaulted while in college.[40] The dynamics of college life appear to fuel the problem, as many survivors are victims of what's called "incapacitated assault": they are sexually abused while drunk, under the influence of drugs, passed out, or otherwise incapacitated.[41] Perpetrators often prey on incapacitated women, and sometimes surreptitiously provide their victims with drugs or alcohol.[42] Perpetrators who drink prior to an assault are more likely to believe that alcohol increases their sex drive – and are also more likely to think that a woman's drinking itself signals that she's interested in sex.[43]

Most college victims are assaulted by someone they know, especially in incapacitated assaults.[44] And parties are often the site of the crime: a 2007 study found that 58% of incapacitated rapes and 28% of forced rapes took place at a party.[45] Notably, campus perpetrators are often serial offenders. One study found that 7% of college men admitted to committing rape or attempted rape, and 63% of these men admitted to committing multiple offenses, averaging six rapes each.[46]

College survivors suffer high rates of PTSD, depression, and drug or alcohol abuse, which can hamper their ability to succeed in school.[47] Depression and anxiety are linked to higher college dropout rates, as is substance abuse.[48]

Reporting rates for campus sexual assault are also very low: on average only 12% of student victims report the assault to law enforcement.[49]

---

[40] The Campus Sexual Assault (CSA) Study (2007); The Campus Sexual Assault Study was conducted by RTI International and funded by the National Institute of Justice. Data were collected using a web-based survey from undergraduate students (5,466 women and 1,375 men) at two large, public universities.; Krebs, C. P., Lindquist, C. H., Warner, T. D., Fisher, B. S., & Martin, S. L (2009) College Women's Experiences with Physically Forced, Alcohol- or Other Drug-Enabled, and Drug-Facilitated Sexual Assault Before and Since Entering College. *Journal of American College Health, 57*(6), 639-647.

[41] Kilpatrick, D. G., Resnick, H. S., Ruggiero, K. J., Conoscenti, L. M., & McCauley, J. (2007). *Drug facilitated, incapacitated, and forcible rape: A national study* (NCJ 219181). Charleston, SC: Medical University of South Carolina, National Crime Victims Research & Treatment Center.[Hereafter cited as Kilpatrick (2007)]

[42] Ibid.

[43] Zawacki, T., Abbey, A., Buck, P. O., McAuslan, P., & Clinton-Sherrod, A. M. (2003). Perpetrators of alcohol-involved sexual assaults: How do they differ from other sexual assault perpetrators and nonperpetrators? *Aggressive Behavior, 29*(4), 366-380.

[44] The Campus Sexual Assault (CSA) Study (2007)

[45] The Campus Sexual Assault (CSA) Study (2007).

[46] Lisak, D., & Miller, P. M. (2002). Repeat Rape and Multiple Offending Among Undetected Rapists. *Violence and Victims, 17*(1), 73-84. [Hereafter cited as Lisak (2002)]

[47] Kilpatrick (2007)

[48] Eisenberg, D., Golberstein, E., & Hunt, J. B. (2009). Mental Health and Academic Success in College. *B E Journal of Economic Analysis & Policy, 9*(1), 1-35.; Arria, A. M., Garnier-Dykstra, L. M., Caldeira, K. M., Vincent, K. B., Winick, E. R., & O'Grady, K. E. (2013). Drug use patterns and continuous enrollment in college: results from a longitudinal study. *Journal of Studies on Alcohol and Drugs, 74*(1), 71-83.

[49] Kilpatrick (2007)

The Economic Costs

Although the economic costs of rape and sexual assault are hard to quantify and the data is limited, the existing research indicates that the costs are great. Various research studies have examined the quantifiable cost per rape, accounting for such costs as medical and victim services, loss of productivity, and law enforcement resources. Researchers also generally agree that intangible costs, such as decreased quality of life, though difficult to monetize, are also a necessary part of the cost calculus for sexual assault. (Many researches, in fact, believe the intangible costs are especially high in cases of sexual assault, due to the serious physical and mental health consequences for survivors.) Each of the studies we examined used a somewhat different methodology, but all found the costs to be significant – ranging from \$87,000 to \$240,776 per rape.[50]

In another study, the National Crime Victimization Survey found that between 2005-2010, 58% of female sexual assault victims were injured, 35% of whom received medical treatment.[51] For women who are raped by an intimate partner, about 36.2% are physically injured and, of those, 31% receive some type of medical care.[52] The injuries for intimate-partner rapes range from scratches, bruises, or welts to lacerations, broken bones, dislocated joints, head or spinal cord injuries, chipped or broken teeth, or internal injuries.[53] Nearly 80% of those who receive medical care are treated in a hospital, and 43.6% of those victims spend one or more nights there.[54]

A 2003 CDC report on the costs of intimate partner violence found that the average medical cost for victims who received treatment was \$2,084 per victimization. In half of these cases, private or group health insurers were the primary source of payment; survivors bore most of the financial burden one-fourth of the time.[55] Many survivors incur at least some out-of-pocket costs for their medical care.

Also among intimate-partner rape survivors, more than one-fifth lose time from paid work, with an average loss of 8.1 days. Additionally, over one-eighth report losing time from household chores, with an average of 13.5 days lost. Nationally, rape survivors lose an estimated 1.1 million days of activity each year.[56]

---

[50] Miller, T.R., Cohen, M.A., & Wiersema, B. (1996). *Victim costs and consequences: A new look.* National Institute of Justice. https://www.ncjrs.gov/pdffiles/victcost.pdf; Delisi, M. (2010). Murder by numbers: Monetary costs imposed by a sample of homicide offenders. *The Journal of Forensic Psychiatry & Psychology, 21,* 501-513.; Cohen, M. A., and Piquero, A.R. (2009) "New Evidence on the Monetary Value of Saving a High Risk Youth," *Journal of Quantitative Criminology, 25*(1), 25–49. French, Michael T., Kathryn E. McCollister, and David Reznik (2010) The Cost of Crime to Society: New Crime-Specific Estimates for Policy and Program Evaluation. *Drug Alcohol Dependence, 108*(1-2), 98-109.

[51] Planty (2013)

[52] NCIPC (2003). Costs of Intimate Partner Violence Against Women in the United States. Department of Health and Human Services, Centers for Disease Control and Prevention, March 2003. [hereafter referred to as NCIPC (2013)].

[53] NCIPC (2003)

[54] NCIPC (2003)

[55] NCIPC (2003)

[56] NCIPC (2003)

The Criminal Justice Response

According to the National Crime Victimization Survey, between 2005-2010, only 36% of rapes or sexual assaults were reported to the police.[57] Male survivors report their assault at even lower rates than women.[58] But even when sexual assaults are reported, many assailants are not arrested and many cases are not prosecuted.

Arrests

Arrest rates for sexual assault cases are low. According to the National Crime Victimization Survey, approximately 12% of the 283,200 annual rape or sexual assault victimizations between 2005-2010 resulted in an arrest at the scene or during a follow-up investigation.[59]

Many factors may contribute to low arrest rates, and these cases can be challenging to investigate. However, research shows that some police officers still believe certain rape myths (e.g., that many women falsely claim rape to get attention), which may help account for the low rates.[60] Similarly, if victims do not behave the way some police officers expect (e.g., crying) an officer may believe she is making a false report[61] – when, in reality, only 2-10% of reported rapes are false.[62]

Sexual assault cases can also be difficult to investigate because of the effects of the trauma itself. Victims of rape and sexual assault sometimes have difficulty recalling the event, and scientific research has found that the trauma after a crime like rape can damage the parts of the brain that control memory.[63] As a result, a victim may have impaired verbal skills, short term memory loss, memory fragmentation, and delayed recall.[64]

---

[57] Planty (2013)

[58] Hart TC, Rennison CM. (2003). *Reporting crime to the police: 1992-2000*. Washington DC: U.S. Bureau of Justice Statistics, U.S. Department of Justice.

[59] Planty (2013); The National Crime Victimization Survey is an annual survey of 90,000 households, comprising nearly 160,000 people. Respondents are asked about the frequency, characteristics, and consequences of criminal victimizations. For more information, visit www.bjs.gov.

[60] Page, A. D. (2008). Judging Women and Defining Crime: Police Officers' Attitudes Toward Women and Rape. *Sociological Spectrum, 28*(4), 389-411.

[61] Bollingmo, Guri C. (2008). Credibility of the emotional witness: A study of ratings by police investigators. *Psychology, Crime & Law, 14*(1), 29-40.

[62] Lisak, D., Gardinier, L., Nicksa, S. C., & Cote, A. M. (2010). False allegation of sexual assault: An analysis of ten years of reported cases. *Violence Against Women, 16*(12), 1318-1334.

[63] Bremner, J.D., Elzinga, B., Schmahl, C., & Vermetten, E. (2008). Structural and functional plasticity of the human brain in posttraumatic stress disorder. *Progress in Brain Research. 167*(1), 171-186.

[64] Nixon, R. D., Nishith, P., & Resick, P. A. (2004). The Accumulative Effect of Trauma Exposure on Short-Term and Delayed Verbal Memory in a Treatment-Seeking Sample of Female Rape Victims. *Journal of Traumatic Stress, 17*(1), 31-35.

Trauma-related memory loss can also mean cases get dropped: preliminary evidence suggests that victims who viewed themselves as giving incoherent accounts to law enforcement were less likely to proceed with their cases.[65]

Whatever the reasons, many victims have lost faith in the system, and believe they were ill-treated by those who should be on their side. Some victims report that law enforcement officers actively discouraged them from reporting, asked questions about their sexual history and dress, and overemphasized prosecution for false reports.[66] Survivors who encounter victim-blaming responses from officials have significantly higher levels of post-traumatic stress than those who do not.[67]

Prosecutions

While national prosecution data is not available, some research suggests that prosecution rates remain low in many jurisdictions.

One study indicated that two-thirds of survivors have had their legal cases dismissed, and more than 80% of the time, this contradicted her desire to prosecute.[68] According to another study of 526 cases in two large cities where sexual assault arrests were made, only about half were prosecuted.[69] Prosecutors were more likely to file charges when physical evidence connecting the suspect to the crime was present, if the suspect had a prior criminal record, and if there were no questions about the survivor's character or behavior.[70]

Rape kit testing. In some jurisdictions, the backlog of untested rape kits may also factor into low prosecution rates. After an assault, victims may seek a forensic exam – called a rape kit – that includes the collection of the perpetrator's DNA and documentation of injuries or other evidence of rape or sexual assault. Although there is not reliable national data, in recent years, media reports have revealed that thousands of rape kits have either not been forwarded to crime labs or are backlogged at the labs waiting to be tested.

---

[65] Hardy, A., Young, K., & Holmes, E. A. (2009). Does trauma memory play a role in the experience of reporting sexual assault during police interviews? An exploratory study. *Memory, 17*(8), 783-788.

[66] Campbell, R. (2006). Rape Survivors' Experiences With the Legal and Medical Systems: Do Rape Victim Advocates Make a Difference? *Violence Against Women, 12*(1), 30-45. [Hereafter cited as Campbell (2006)]; Logan, T., Evans, L., Stevenson, E., & Jordan, C. E. (2005). Barriers to Services for Rural and Urban Survivors of Rape. *Journal of Interpersonal Violence, 20*(5), 591-616.

[67] Campbell, R., & Raja, S. (2005). The sexual assault and secondary victimization of female veterans: Help-seeking experiences in military and civilian social systems. Psychology of Women Quarterly, 29, 97–106.

[68] Campbell, R., Wasco, S.M., Ahrens, C.E., Sefl, T., & Barnes, H.E. (2001). Preventing the "Second Rape": Rape Survivors' Experiences with Community Service Providers. *Journal of Interpersonal* Violence, 16(12).; Campbell, R. (1998). The community response to rape: Victims'experiences with the legal, medical, and mental health systems. *American Journal of Community Psychology, 26*(3), 355-379.

[69] Spohn, C. & Holleran, D. (2004). *Prosecuting sexual assault: A comparison of charging decisions in sexual assault cases involving strangers, acquaintances, and intimate partners* (NCJ 199720). Washington, DC: National Institute of Justice, U.S. Department of Justice.

[70] Ibid.

Testing of rape kits can be vital for the prosecution of cases. When a rape kit is tested, a unique DNA profile can often be identified and submitted to the FBI's Combined DNA Index System (CODIS). This software platform includes nationwide DNA samples from crime scenes, convicted offenders, and arrestees. In this way, crimes like rape and sexual assault can be matched to other samples in the database, identifying assailants and linking crimes together.

Law enforcement policies governing which kits should be prioritized for testing are inconsistent. In a survey of over 2,000 law enforcement agencies, 44% reported that one reason they did not send forensic evidence to a laboratory was because the suspect had not been identified; 15% said they did not submit the evidence because a prosecutor didn't request it, and 11% cited the lab's inability to produce timely results.[71] Even when law enforcement submits the kit to a crime lab, in some jurisdictions, the evidence remains untested for many months.

Crime labs have struggled over the past decade to meet the demand for DNA testing for all types of crimes. And while labs were able to process 10% more cases in 2011 than in 2009, they also received 16.4% more requests for DNA testing.[72] And with demand continuing to outpace capacity, the rape kit backlog may continue to grow.

---

[71] Ritter, N. (2011). *The road ahead : unanalyzed evidence in sexual assault cases.* Washington, DC: U.S. Dept. of Justice, Office of Justice Programs, National Institute of Justice. [Hereafter referred to as Ritter (2011)]
[72] Nelson, M ,et. al. (2013). *Making Sense of DNA Backlogs: Myths Vs. Reality.* Washington, DC: National Institute of Justice, Office of Justice Programs, U.S. Dept. of Justice.

Taking Action to Break the Cycle of Violence

On October 27, 2010, the White House Council on Women and Girls and the Office of the Vice President held the first national roundtable on sexual assault. Advocates, researchers, survivors, and federal officials came together to discuss the problem and the federal government's role in helping bring an end to this violence. As a result of the roundtable, federal agencies have undertaken unprecedented efforts to address rape and sexual assault.

The White House Council on Women and Girls and the Office of the Vice President also co-host an interagency working group on violence against women. This is a first-of-its kind forum for collaboration and information-sharing among key federal agencies about best practices to prevent sexual assault and to provide support for victims. This interagency group formulated recommendations for reauthorization of the Violence Against Women Act and developed other initiatives to respond to President Obama's call for action.

Vice President Joe Biden speaks at the National Domestic Violence Hotline, in Austin, Texas, Oct. 30, 2013. (Official White House Photo by David Lienemann)

The Violence Against Women Act

The Violence Against Women Act forms the backbone of our nation's response to domestic violence, dating violence, rape, sexual assault and stalking. Authored by then-Senator Biden, and first enacted in 1994, VAWA addresses the problem on multiple fronts: among its many original provisions, VAWA created new, tough penalties for abusers, sex offenders and stalkers (and prompted many states to revise their codes); strengthened victims' abilities to get and enforce protection orders; provided incentives for more arrests, investigations and prosecutions of these crimes; gave survivors new access to legal representation; encouraged communities to develop special multidisciplinary domestic violence response teams; and provided unprecedented resources to states, local, and tribal governments and non-profit organizations to provide services for survivors. Since passage of VAWA, annual rates of domestic violence have dropped by 64%.[73]

In recent years, VAWA has expanded to focus even more particularly on sexual assault. In 2005, VAWA created the Sexual Assault Services Program (SASP), the first funding stream to focus specifically on direct services and advocacy for victims of rape and sexual assault. And in March 2013, President Obama signed the third reauthorization of VAWA, which made additional changes in the law, and brought new resources to bear on the problem.

VAWA 2013 includes set-aside funding and new purpose areas for multidisciplinary sexual assault response teams, sexual assault nurse examiner programs (SANE), specialized law enforcement units, and training for criminal justice professionals. This new focus will encourage states and local law enforcement agencies to adopt practices that have proven effective in holding sexual assault offenders accountable. The Justice Department provides technical assistance and support to states as they work to scale up these practices.

The Obama Administration also worked with Congress to ensure that VAWA addresses the needs of victims who have historically been overlooked. VAWA 2013 included new protections for LGBT victims and encourages states to develop services for LGBT communities. Despite opposition from some in Congress, the Administration also successfully fought to protect the U visa program that allows immigrant victims to safely report crimes, including sexual assault. VAWA 2013 also included a landmark provision recognizing the authority of tribes to prosecute domestic violence crimes committed on tribal lands regardless of the race of the perpetrator.

To address the link between violence and housing instability, VAWA 2013 included new protections for sexual assault survivors in public and other subsidized housing. Among other housing protections, the law requires that survivors of domestic violence, dating violence, sexual assault and stalking be permitted to transfer to other available housing if necessary. Since most sexual assaults occur in or near the survivor's residence, this provision can be essential to helping survivors reestablish a sense of safety and security. The Department of Housing and Urban Development (HUD) has issued a notice to

---

[73] Catalano, S. (2012). Intimate Partner Violence, 1993-2010. U.S. Department of Justice. Bureau of Justice Statistics.; Additionally, VAWA has reduced crimes and the subsequent costs to the criminal justice and health care systems. One study found that VAWA saved an estimated $12.6 billion in net averted social costs in its first 6 years alone. Clark, K. A, Biddle, A., & Martin, S. (2002). A cost-benefit analysis of the Violence Against Women Act of 1994. *Violence Against Women, 8*(4), 417-428; Erratum. *Violence Against Women, 9*(1), 136.

housing providers participating in HUD programs covered by VAWA about these new protections and is engaged in rule-making to implement them.

VAWA 2013 also recognized that certain populations – notably teens and Native American women – are particularly vulnerable to sex trafficking, and authorizes funds to serve these victims.

Supporting Victims/Survivors

Over the past four years, and at the Administration's urging, Congress doubled funding for VAWA's Sexual Assault Services Program (SASP). Under SASP, and among other services, local rape crisis centers, mental health professionals, and social service providers help survivors navigate the criminal justice system. This approach is supported by research: survivors who have assistance from an advocate are more likely to have police reports taken and less likely to be treated poorly by officers.[74] Survivors also report less distress after contact with the legal system and upon receiving medical care.[75]

SASP also reaches well beyond the criminal justice system – for its grantees serve victims whether or not they choose to report a crime. Even at its best, the criminal justice system is a limited remedy for the harm many victims have suffered. Thus, SASP grantees also provide the emotional and practical support survivors need to rebuild their lives – such as crisis intervention, counseling, 24-hour sexual assault hotlines, and advocacy at various steps of the road to recovery. Notably, a growing number of survivors served by this program are adults who were victimized as children and who are only now able to disclose what happened to them and find help.

Local rape crisis centers report that the current demand for services is outpacing their ability to serve those in need. According to the National Alliance to End Sexual Violence, one-third of rape crisis centers have waiting lists for counseling services, and in some cases the wait is as long as two months.[76]

With VAWA funding, DOJ's Office on Violence Against Women (OVW) has launched the Sexual Assault Demonstration Initiative in six sites to improve victim services in areas where there is not a specialized rape crisis center. By 2015, this project is expected to provide lessons and models that can be replicated in other communities.

In addition to VAWA funding, the Administration makes important investments in direct services for victims under the Victims of Crime Act (VOCA) Victim Assistance and Victim Compensation programs. These funds support delivery of crisis intervention, counseling, criminal justice advocacy, and compensation for victims of many types of

---

[74] Campbell (2006)
[75] Ibid.
[76] "2013 Rape Crisis Center Survey." National Alliance to End Sexual Violence. Accessed from: http://endsexualviolence.org/where-we-stand/2013-rape-crisis-center-survey.

crimes, including rape and sexual assault. The Justice Department's Office of Victims of Crime (OVC) prioritizes sexual assault, and approximately 15% of VOCA Victim Assistance funding supports direct services to sexual assault victims.

Improving the Criminal Justice System

To reduce rape and sexual assault, offenders must be held accountable. Otherwise, a broad cycle of violence continues: perpetrators of sexual assault are commonly repeat offenders, who commit both multiple rapes and other crimes.[77] The strongest predictor of sexual assault is a previous sexual assault, which makes rape a particularly crucial crime to prosecute.[78]

Among other measures, the Department of Justice is working to increase arrest and conviction rates by supporting multidisciplinary sexual assault teams; these are specially trained law enforcement officers, detectives, prosecutors, healthcare providers and victim advocates, all working together to support survivors and increase the odds of successful prosecutions. These specialized units have proven effective in combatting domestic violence and are a promising model for addressing sexual assault. The evidence collected by specialized units is more likely to be useful for prosecution, leading to higher rates of prosecution, conviction, and sentencing.[79] In VAWA-funded specialized units, sexual assault conviction rates are much higher than average, from 60-80%.

Specialized training for law enforcement and prosecutors. The trauma caused by a sexual assault can affect a victim's ability to interact with law enforcement, recall events, and manage emotions. When law enforcement officers understand the physiological effects of trauma, they can better elicit information from victims and understand their behavior. OVW is partnering with the International Association of Chiefs of Police (IACP) to provide training for law enforcement agencies on how to conduct trauma-informed sexual assault interviews and investigations.

Training for prosecutors is equally important. Through a cooperative agreement with the organization AEquitas ("The Prosecutors' Resource on Violence Against Women"), OVW supports a range of technical assistance and training to help prosecutors better take on sexual assault cases. AEquitas hosts several national training events, conducts legal research, and provides prosecutors with around-the-clock case consultation.

---

[77] Abbey, A., Parkhill, M., Clinton-Sherrod, A. M., Zawacki, T. (2007). A Comparison of Men Who Committed Different Types of Sexual Assault in a Community Sample. *Journal of Interpersonal Violence, 22*(12), 1567-580.; Lisak, D., & Miller, P (2002). Repeat Rape and Multiple Offending Among Undetected Rapists. *Violence and Victims,* 17, 73-84.

[78] Loh, C., Gidycz, C., Lobo, T., Luthra, R. (2005). A Prospective Analysis of Sexual Assault Perpetration Risk Factors Related to Perpetrator Characteristics. *Journal of Interpersonal Violence,* 20(10), 1325-348.

[79] Jolin, A., Feyerherm, W., Fountain, R., & Friedman, S. (1998). *Beyond arrest: The Portland, Oregon domestic violence experiment, final report* (No. NCJRS 179968). Washington, DC: U.S. Department of Justice

Sexual assault forensic evidence. A key factor in improving prosecution rates for rape and sexual assault is the proper collection of forensic evidence – and the Administration has made significant advances on several fronts.

In April 2013, the Justice Department released a revised version of the National Protocol for Sexual Assault Medical Forensic Examinations (SAFE Protocol, 2d). The SAFE Protocol provides a best-practices guide to conducting medical forensic examinations and promotes high-quality, sensitive, and supportive exams for survivors of rape and sexual assault. The updated SAFE Protocol includes information on assisting populations with special needs such as survivors with limited English proficiency; survivors with disabilities; American Indian and Alaska Native victims; military personnel; and lesbian, gay, bisexual, or transgender victims. The SAFE Protocol is available at the National Criminal Justice Reference Service website at:
https://www.ncjrs.gov/pdffiles1/ovw/241903.pdf.

Sexual Assault Nurse Examiners (SANEs) can also be key to effective evidence collection. These nurse examiners are trained to provide respectful and supportive care while collecting forensic evidence after a rape or sexual assault. In addition to improving victim care, SANE programs (like those funded by OVW's STOP Program) enhance the quality of forensic evidence, improve law enforcement's ability to collect information and file charges, and increase rates of successful prosecutions.[80] VAWA rural grants are also funding SANEs to conduct forensic exams, collect evidence, and provide health care to victims in rural communities.

The Justice Department is also using telemedicine technology to improve the collection of evidence. Its Office for Victims of Crime partnered with the National Institute of Justice to establish a National Sexual Assault TeleNursing Center at the Massachusetts Department of Public Health. The Center will provide 24/7, year-round remote expert consultation by SANEs to clinicians caring for adult and adolescent sexual assault patients. The three-year cooperative agreement will establish pilot projects at two military medical facilities to perform telemedicine consultation during sexual assault forensic exams. The Center is expected to be fully operational in 2015, and the project will be expanded to include telemedicine sites in Indian country, rural communities, and prisons.

Rape kit backlog. Once forensic evidence has been collected, it needs to be tested for DNA – and this Administration has worked proactively to address the nation's backlog of rape kits.

---

[80] Campbell, R., Patterson, D., & Bybee, D. (2011). Using mixed methods to evaluate a community intervention for sexual assault survivors: A methodological tale. *Violence Against Women, 17*(3), 376–388.; Campbell, R., Bybee, D., Ford, J., & Patterson, D. (2008). *Systems change analysis of SANE programs: Identifying the mediating mechanisms of criminal justice system impact* (No. NCJRS 226497). Washington, DC: U.S. Department of Justice.; Nugent-Borakove, E., Fanflik, P., Johnson, N., Burgess, A., & O'Connor, A. L. (2006). *Testing the efficacy of SANE/SART programs: Do they make a difference in sexual assault arrest and prosecution outcomes?* Washington, DC: Department of Justice.

Through its DNA Backlog Reduction Program, the National Institute of Justice (NIJ) funds 120 state and local crime labs to conduct DNA testing from crime scenes and convicted offenders. Rape kits are included in this testing program, but, as noted, law enforcement investigators sometimes don't prioritize these kits for forwarding to a lab. Time has shown, however, that DNA is a powerful tool to link crimes together and create new investigative leads in rape cases.

In 2011, NIJ funded pilot projects in Detroit and Houston to inventory their untested kits and develop protocols for submitting these kits to crime labs. Final reports are due later this year, but preliminary results from Detroit show what can happen when old rape kits are tested: from a sample of 569 kits, 32 serial offenders were identified and five prosecutions initiated. One of the lessons from this project, however, is that testing alone is not enough; when jurisdictions test large volumes of rape kits, they also need the resources to follow-up on the leads – which means having trained detectives, victim advocates, and prosecutors available and working together to successfully pursue the new cases.

Other cities have taken on their untested kits with mixed results, and NIJ continues to study the causes of backlogs and effectiveness of testing programs. NIJ is examining the value of testing rape kits from various types of crimes, including stranger, acquaintance, and intimate partner rapes. In some of these circumstances, the DNA evidence may not be the key to solving that specific crime, but it can create new investigative leads in cold cases and help identify serial offenders. The NIJ research projects are designed to examine the efficacy and criminal justice outcomes of testing rape kits from various types of assaults.

Another lesson learned from the pilot projects is that survivors have different feelings about having their rape kits tested. Survivors have often worked hard to overcome the effects of a rape and put their lives back together. The prospect of having an old kit tested can bring a flood of emotion: some survivors may still be interested in pursuing justice, while others find the toll of reopening old wounds too high. NIJ and OVW are researching and exploring approaches to reducing rape kit backlogs that account for survivors' rights, needs, and preferences – and specifically, how to notify survivors and involve them in the criminal justice process.

Combating Sexual Assault on Campus

The Federal Government enforces several laws that oblige educational institutions to combat campus sexual assault. Title IX requires schools receiving federal funding to take necessary steps to prevent sexual assault on their campuses, and to respond quickly and effectively when an assault occurs. The Clery Act requires colleges and universities that participate in federal financial aid programs to report annual statistics on crime on or near their campuses, to develop and disseminate prevention policies, and to ensure victims their basic rights.[81]

This Administration has undertaken a major effort to better enforce the laws addressing rape and sexual assault at educational institutions. In 2011, Vice President Biden and Education Secretary Duncan announced new guidance to help schools, colleges and universities understand their obligations under Title IX. As a result of the guidance, students also have a better understanding about their schools' responsibilities – and, not coincidentally, Title IX complaints are on the rise and student activists are increasingly holding schools more accountable.

The Department of Education's Office for Civil Rights (OCR) is charged with administratively enforcing Title IX in schools. OCR may initiate an investigation either proactively or based on a student's formal complaint. If schools are found to violate Title IX, they can be denied federal funds – although OCR must first seek to voluntarily resolve the non-compliance before terminating funds. Through this voluntary resolution process, OCR has entered into agreements that require schools to develop, among other things:

- Comprehensive plans for educating students and employees about sexual assault;
- Policies and practices for responding to allegations of sexual violence;
- Adequate training for school officials charged with responding to complaints; and
- Policies to ensure that survivors are given the remedies and resources they need to continue their educations.

The Department of Justice, upon referrals from other agencies, can initiate litigation to require schools to better address campus sexual assaults. As noted, the Department has a number of tools in its toolbox – including Title IX, Title IV of the Civil Rights Act, and the Safe Streets Act – that it can use to bring all facets of a school, as well as local police departments, into compliance with the law.

VAWA 2013 amended the Clery Act to mandate that schools develop new initiatives to respond to domestic violence, dating violence, sexual assault and stalking. The new law also strengthens existing provisions in the Clery Act, requiring institutions to bolster prevention education programs for students and employees, and to establish procedures for responding to incidents of sexual violence on campus. To implement these changes, the Department of Education is engaging in negotiated rule-making with the goal of publishing a final rule by November 2014. The Department is committed to transparency in the rule-making process, and has included advocacy groups and educational associations in this endeavor.

---

[81] Several other laws also authorize the Justice Department to investigate campus sexual assaults and to help schools adopt comprehensive policies and practices to address the problem. These include Title IV of the Civil Rights Act of 1964; the Violent Crime Control and Law Enforcement Act of 1994, 42 U.S.C. § 14141 ("Section 14141"); and the Omnibus Crime Control and Safe Streets Act of 1968, 42 U.S.C. 3789d ("Safe Streets Act").

The Department of Education's Federal Student Aid (FSA) office is responsible for enforcing the Clery Act, and conducts on-site reviews to ensure schools' compliance with the Act. If an institution is found to have violated the Clery Act, FSA directs it to take steps to come into compliance and can impose fines for violations.

The Justice Department's Office on Violence Against Women administers VAWA grants that help colleges and universities create holistic responses to sexual assault on campus, including offering victim services, implementing prevention programs, training campus law enforcement, and working with school administrators to improve the student disciplinary process.

Because campus sexual assault is the subject of intersecting federal laws, policies, and grant programs, it is a key area for improved interagency collaboration. And it is in that spirit that, on January 22, 2014, President Obama created the White House Task Force to Protect Students from Sexual Assault. The objectives of the task force are to:

- Provide educational institutions with best practices for preventing and responding to rape and sexual assault.
- Build on the federal government's enforcement efforts to ensure that educational institutions comply fully with their legal obligations.
- Improve transparency of the government's enforcement activities.
- Increase the public's awareness of an institution's track record in addressing rape and sexual assault.
- Enhance coordination among federal agencies to hold schools accountable if they do not confront sexual violence on their campuses.

Reaching Teens and Young Adults

In 2011, Vice President Biden developed the **1 is 2 Many Campaign** to focus on dating violence and sexual assault suffered by teens and young women. As part of this initiative, the Vice President solicited ideas from college students nationwide about how to prevent violence on campus. An overwhelming number of respondents said one thing: get men involved. Consequently, in a series of regional forums, federal agencies and communities came together to engage men in the effort to end violence against women.

The **1 is 2 Many Campaign** also recognizes that technology can be a powerful tool to help prevent dating violence and sexual assault. In 2011, Vice President Biden and Health and Human Services Secretary Sebelius issued an "app challenge" that inspired two award-winning mobile apps especially geared toward young people. One of these apps – Circle of 6 – puts a group of friends instantly in touch with each other – so someone in trouble can send a "come and get me" message, complete with a GPS map to show her exact location. This app has been downloaded in 27 countries and was recently adapted for use in India.

Also in 2011, in response to the Vice President's call to action, the Justice Department funded the National Dating Abuse Helpline, which gives teens and young adults access to services (such as counseling and information about where to turn) in a way that they are most comfortable – via text messaging and online "chats." The Justice Department continues to support these digital services.

Working with schools. As part of **1 is 2 Many**, Vice President Biden also convened parents, teachers, educational associations, youth groups, and school counselors to raise awareness about teen dating violence and sexual assault. These groups were eager to help, but asked for additional guidance on what schools could do. In response, the Department of Education sent a "Dear Colleague" letter in 2013 to school districts across the country, urging them to address gender-based violence, including sexual assault, and to provide training to school personnel – from bus drivers to school nurses – who may witness such violence. The letter included a resource packet on teen dating violence with information on school-based policies and practices that have proven effective. New research has found that school and classroom-based intervention programs can reduce the incidence of teen dating violence and sexual harassment by up to 50 percent.[82]

Working with men to change social norms. Social norms research reveals that men often overestimate other men's acceptance of abusive behavior towards women and underestimate other men's willingness to intervene when a woman is in trouble.[83] When men and boys believe that their peers accept sexist and abusive behavior, they are much less likely to help. That, in turn, can lead perpetrators to think their actions are acceptable – which, of course, perpetuates the violence. Research additionally shows that peer attitudes toward sexual aggression have a significant influence on men's willingness to intervene – which means that when men speak out against abuse, other men are more likely to step in to neutralize a risky situation and prevent an assault.[84]

Bystander intervention training seeks to engage men and boys as allies rather than would-be perpetrators. It acknowledges that most men are not assailants and that everyone can help stop the violence. This sort of training also builds men's confidence and ability to take action – like preventing or interrupting an assault; speaking out against rape acceptance myths (e.g., women want to be raped and "ask for it"); and supporting survivors. Bystander intervention is integrated throughout the U.S. military's prevention activities, and is also increasingly being taught on college campuses.

The CDC's Rape Prevention and Education (RPE) program also funds efforts by states and territories to prevent sexual assault. RPE grantees are currently engaged in a range of

---

[82] Taylor, B, Stein, N.D., Woods, D., Mumford, E. (2011) *Shifting Boundaries: Final Report on an Experimental Evaluation of a Youth Dating Violence Prevention Program in New York City Middle Schools* No. NCJRS 236175). Washington, DC: U.S. Department of Justice.

[83] Berkowitz, A.D. (2010) "Fostering Healthy Norms to Prevent Violence and Abuse: The Social Norms Approach." Accessed from: http://www.alanberkowitz.com/articles/Preventing%20Sexual%20Violence%20Chapter%20-%20Revision.pdf

[84] Brown, A.L. & Messman-Moore, T.L. (2010) Personal and Perceived Peer Attitudes Supporting Sexual Aggression as Predictors of Male College Students' Willingness to Intervene Against Sexual Aggression. *Journal of Interpersonal Violence, 25*(3) 503-517.

activities, including implementing culturally relevant prevention strategies based on best practices, conducting training, and expanding the prevention message through creative partnerships. Grantees are working with coaches, boys, men, and the entertainment industry to develop innovative prevention strategies. CDC is also funding research grants to rigorously evaluate promising practices, strategies, and policies for their impact on rates of sexual violence.

In 2011, the Department of Justice launched the VAWA Engaging Men in Preventing Sexual Assault and Domestic Violence program – which funds multi-faceted strategies to engage men as allies and influencers of other men. Using social media combined with hands-on mentorship, the program aims to develop new male leaders willing to speak up about violence against women and girls.

Addressing sex trafficking. Yong people are among those most vulnerable to human trafficking, and runaway, homeless, and LGBT youth are at particular risk.[85] In January 2014, the Administration released the Federal Strategic Action Plan on Services for Victims of Human Trafficking in the United States. This five-year plan lays a path for further coordination, collaboration, and capacity across governmental and nongovernmental entities to support survivors of human trafficking, including youth. The Federal Strategic Action Plan is available here: http://www.ovc.gov/pubs/FederalHumanTraffickingStrategicPlan.pdf

Addressing the intersection between HIV/AIDS, violence against women, and gender-related health disparities.

Over half of women living with HIV in the United States have been raped, assaulted, or stalked by an intimate partner – which is considerably higher than the national rate among women overall (56% vs. 36%).[86] Recognizing that violence against women and girls is a driving factor in the domestic HIV/AIDS epidemic, President Obama created an interagency Federal Working Group in 2012 to study this issue, as well as gender-related health disparities. Co-chaired by the White House Advisor on Violence Against Women and the Director of the Office of National AIDS Policy, the Working Group developed 56 action items for agencies across the Federal government – including ways for agencies to better respond to the health needs of women who have been raped or sexually assaulted, and linking primary prevention strategies for intimate partner violence with efforts to prevent the transmission of HIV. The Working Group Report can be accessed here: http://www.whitehouse.gov/sites/default/files/docs/vaw-hiv_working_group_report_final_-_9-6--2013.pdf

---

[85] Clawson, H.J., Dutch, M., Solomon, A., & Goldblatt Grace, L. (2009). Human Trafficking Into and Within the United States: A Review of the Literature. Washington, DC.: Office of the Assistant Secretary for Planning and Evaluation (ASPE), U.S. Department of Health and Human Services.
[86] Machtinger, E.L., et al. Psychological trauma and PTSD in HIV-positive women: a meta-analysis. *AIDS Behavior.* 2012; 16(8): 2091-2100. ; NISVS (2010)

Responding to Sexual Assault in the Military

Our military members continue to face the threat of sexual assault within their ranks and the Administration bears a unique responsibility to protect the women and men in uniform who dedicate their lives to protecting our nation. The President is committed to addressing this corrosive problem, which destroys trust among our troops and undermines our readiness. Over the past year, the Department of Defense (DOD), in collaboration with the White House, has developed a set of executive actions, legislative proposals, and training programs to more effectively prevent and respond to sexual assault in the military.

Secretary Hagel has directed a series of executive actions that will improve command accountability, expand victims' rights within the military justice system, and improve victim treatment by their peers, co-workers, and chains of command. Most notably, Secretary Hagel directed each service to provide legal counsel for all victims of sexual assault. This landmark reform will ensure that victims are provided with personalized legal advice and representation throughout the legal process. DOD has also developed a new curriculum for sexual assault prevention and response training. This training is being provided to new recruits, officers preparing to assume command, and senior enlisted personnel, and is now expanding to reach all members of the force.

DOD developed and submitted to Congress two legislative proposals aimed at reforming the Uniform Code of Military Justice. These proposals – which were included in the National Defense Reauthorization Act – will limit the ability of commanders to overturn court-martial findings and reform the pre-trial investigation process to provide greater protections for victims.

In December 2013, President Obama instructed Secretary Hagel and Joint Chiefs of Staff Chairman Dempsey to continue their intensive focus on this issue and directed them to conduct a full-scale review of their progress by December 2014. Based on the results of this report, the President and DOD will consider additional reforms that may be required to eliminate this crime from the ranks and protect the men and women who serve our nation.

Protecting American Indian and Alaska Native Women

President Obama is committed to improving safety in Indian country. In 2009, the Department of Justice launched a new effort to reduce the high rates of crime on Indian reservations, with a particular focus on violence against women. In July 2010, the President signed the Tribal Law and Order Act, bringing new resources to build infrastructure for tribal court systems and encouraging the hiring of more law enforcement officers for Indian lands. Also, the law enhances tribes' authority to prosecute and punish criminals, and authorizes new guidelines for handling sexual assault and domestic violence crimes, from training for law enforcement and court officers, to boosting conviction rates through better evidence collection, to providing better and more comprehensive services to victims.

Prosecuting crimes in Indian country. The Tribal Law and Order Act also encourages United States Attorney's Offices (USAOs) to designate tribal prosecutors as Special Assistant U.S. Attorneys (SAUSA). As a result, many USAOs with Indian country responsibility now have tribal SAUSAs who may prosecute cases in federal court. And in 2012, OVW launched a Tribal Special Assistant United States Attorney Pilot Project, funding eligible tribal prosecutors to pursue violence against women cases in both tribal and federal courts and to enhance collaboration between tribal officials and federal prosecutors. Tailored to meet the particular needs of each participating tribe, this pilot project is designed to improve the quality of cases, the coordination of resources, and the communication of priorities both within and between the various law enforcement agencies working in these jurisdictions. The Justice Department's prioritization of Indian country crime has made a difference: from FY2009-FY2012, prosecutions have increased nearly 54 percent.[87]

VAWA protections. VAWA 2013 also contains provisions that significantly improve the safety of Native women by, among other things, giving federal and tribal law enforcement agencies more authority to hold perpetrators of domestic violence accountable. The tribal provisions in VAWA closed three significant legal gaps by: (1) recognizing certain tribes' power to exercise concurrent criminal jurisdiction over domestic violence cases, regardless of whether the defendant is Indian or non-Indian; (2) clarifying that tribal courts have full civil jurisdiction to issue and enforce protection orders involving any person, Indian or non-Indian; and (3) creating new federal laws to address crimes of violence, such as strangulation, committed against a spouse or intimate partner and providing more robust federal sentences for certain acts of domestic violence in Indian Country.

Leading by Example in the Workplace

For some survivors, the effects of sexual assault can follow them to their jobs. If the perpetrator was a co-worker or the assault occurred near the workplace, the survivor may have ongoing safety concerns. Survivors may need time off from work to attend court hearings, go to counseling, or address other issues related to the assault. Employers can help by developing policies that address safety, use of leave, and other assistance that survivors may need to get their lives back on track.

In April 2012, President Obama directed federal agencies to develop policies to assist victims of domestic violence, sexual assault and stalking in the federal workforce. Led by the Office of Personnel Management (OPM), an interagency workgroup evaluated how sexual assault affects victims in the workplace, and worked closely with agencies to

---

[87] www.justice.gov/tribal/tloa-report-cy-2011-2012.pdf

develop responsive policies. In February 2013, OPM issued "Guidance for Agency-Specific Domestic Violence, Sexual Assault, and Stalking Policies," which provides agencies with guidance to fulfill the goals identified by the President.[88]

Reducing Rape in Prisons

In accordance with the Prison Rape Elimination Act of 2003 (PREA), the Department of Justice released a final rule in May 2012 that requires prisons and other detention facilities to prevent, detect, and respond to sexual assault. Four types of facilities are covered: adult prisons and jails, lockups, community confinement facilities, and juvenile facilities. This regulation is the first federal effort to set standards for all facilities at the local, state, and federal levels to protect incarcerated individuals from sexual abuse. Facilities must develop and maintain zero-tolerance policies regarding sexual abuse, and must also make sure that at-risk populations, including youth, LGBT, and female prisoners, are protected. The Justice Department also released a protocol to improve responses to sexual assault in prisons and other correctional facilities, which is available at: http://ovw.usdoj.gov/docs/confinement-safe-protocol.pdf.

Improving Data Collection

Collecting data on sensitive issues like rape and sexual assault can be challenging. Language, definitions, and survey methods all make a difference in how individuals understand and disclose what has happened to them. The federal government uses various measures to capture the extent of rape and sexual assault, and each takes a different approach. The Administration has been working for several years to enhance and improve data collection in this area.

Uniform Crime Report. The FBI collects data on rapes that are reported to law enforcement through the Uniform Crime Report. Until recently, the definition of rape used to collect this data was very narrow and outdated, and covered only forcible male penile penetration of a female vagina. Nearly all criminal codes have broader definitions, but states have only been required to report crimes meeting this narrow definition. In 2012, the Justice Department modernized its definition to include the various forms of assault now understood to be rape. Among other things, the new definition covers instances where a victim is incapable of consent (e.g., because of drugs or alcohol), is not gender-specific, and includes oral and anal penetration. Because the new definition is more inclusive, reported crimes of rape are likely to rise in future years. As Vice President Biden noted at the time: "Rape is a devastating crime and we can't solve it unless we know the full extent of it."

---

[88] Office of Personnel Management, Guidance for Agency-Specific Domestic Violence, Sexual Assault, and Stalking Policies,"Retrieved from: http://www.opm.gov/policy-data-oversight/worklife/reference-materials/guidance-for-agency-specific-dvsas-policies.pdf.

National Crime Victimization Survey. A second measure of rape comes from the National Crime Victimization Survey (NCVS). Through in-person interviews and follow-up phone calls, this survey collects information about various types of crimes the participants may have experienced in the prior six months. Official estimates of rape in the NCVS have typically been lower than estimates from other governmental surveys and academic research. A panel of experts recently studied NCVS and identified possible reasons for this, including lack of privacy for interviews and the fact that questions are framed in terms of criminal acts rather than behaviors.

The Bureau of Justice Statistics (BJS), which has responsibility for NCVS, has committed to a multiyear project to better understand the possible reasons for the underestimation of rape and sexual assault in the NCVS. Toward that end, BJS is undertaking a major effort to develop and test survey designs for collecting data on rape and sexual assault. This study of 18,100 respondents will compare methods for collecting data about rape and sexual assault on the phone, in-person, and by computer. Data collection will begin in July 2014 and the project is expected to be completed by December 2015.

National Intimate Partner and Sexual Violence Survey. In 2010, CDC launched the National Intimate Partner and Sexual Violence Survey (NISVS). This random-digit-dial survey uses a public health approach in which respondents are asked about specific behaviors they may have experienced in their lifetimes and over the past year. The survey collects lifetime and 12-month prevalence data on sexual violence, stalking, and intimate partner violence. In addition, the survey collects information on the age at the time of the first victimization, demographic characteristics of respondents, demographic characteristics of perpetrators (age, sex, race/ethnicity) and detailed information about the patterns and impact of the violence by specific perpetrators. The survey also gathers information on long-term physical and mental health consequences that may be associated with violence.

Conclusion

Despite the important and unprecedented work being done, there is much more to do. And the problems outlined in this report also provide a roadmap for further action.

As noted, women at our nation's colleges and universities are at particular risk of being sexually assaulted. To make our campuses safer, change needs to come from many quarters: schools must adopt better policies and practices to prevent these crimes and to more effectively respond when they happen – both by holding offenders accountable and giving victims the help they need to physically and emotionally recover. And federal agencies must better ensure that schools are living up to their obligations.

Across all demographics, rapists and sex offenders are too often not made to pay for their crimes, and remain free to assault again. Arrest rates are low and meritorious cases are still being dropped – many times because law enforcement officers and prosecutors are not fully trained on the nature of these crimes or how best to investigate and prosecute them. Many new and promising interviewing, investigative and prosecution protocols are being developed, with cutting-edge science about victim trauma informing the enterprise. We need to further develop these best practices and help get them out to the field.

We can also help local jurisdictions move rape kits off the shelves and into crime labs for testing – so more rapists can be identified through DNA and brought to justice.

This Administration, as noted, has made an unparalleled commitment to getting victims and survivors the many services they need – from crisis intervention, counseling, legal advocacy, medical help, social services, and job and housing assistance – and with a special eye on particularly vulnerable populations. Even so, the demand for these services continues to outpace the supply. We cannot retreat, but must recommit to getting these vital resources to those who need them.

And, of course, we must – and can – continue to change our nation's attitudes about these crimes. Sexual assault is pervasive because our culture still allows it to persist. According to the experts, violence prevention can't just focus on the perpetrators and the survivors. It has to involve everyone. And in order to put an end to this violence, we as a nation must see it for what it is: a crime. Not a misunderstanding, not a private matter, not anyone's right or any woman's fault. And bystanders must be taught and emboldened to step in to stop it. As then Senator Biden said when he was first drafting the Violence Against Women Act:

> "Through this process, I have become convinced that violence against women reflects as much a failure of our nation's collective moral imagination as it does the failure of our nation's laws and regulations. We are helpless to change the

course of this violence unless, and until, we achieve a national consensus that it deserves our profound public outrage."

The Vice President's words ring as true today as they did then.